FIRST PAST THE POST

Verbal Reasoning:

Cloze Tests

Mixed Format

Book 1

© 2013 ElevenPlusExams.co.uk   COPYING STRICTLY PROHIBITED

How to use this book to make the most of 11 plus exam preparation

It is important to remember that for 11 plus exams there is no national syllabus, no pass mark and no retake option. It is therefore vital that your child is fully primed to perform to the best of their ability so that they give themselves the best possible chance on the day.

Unlike similar publications, the **First Past The Post®** series uniquely assesses your child's performance on a question-by-question basis, helping to identify areas for improvement and providing suggestions for further targeted tests. By entering the unique Peer-Compare access code for this book on our website, your child's performance can be compared anonymously to that of others who have taken the same tests.

Verbal Reasoning: Cloze Tests

Cloze tests are passages with missing words or letters which require the child to recognise and select the answer from a set of several options, or to complete the word with the correct spelling. They are designed to test a child's vocabulary and spelling.

This book covers the three main question styles of cloze tests: Word Bank, Multiple Choice and Partial Words.

Never has it been more useful to learn from mistakes!

Students can improve by as much as 15%, not only by focused practice, but also by targeting any weak areas.

How to manage your child's practice

To get the most up-to-date information, visit our website, www.elevenplusexams.co.uk, the UK's largest online resource for 11 plus, with over 65,000 webpages and a forum administered by a select group of experienced moderators.

About the authors

The Eleven Plus Exams' **First Past The Post®** series has been created by a team of experienced tutors and authors from leading British universities.

Published by Technical One Ltd t/a Eleven Plus Exams

With special thanks to the children who tested our material at the ElevenPlusExams centre in Harrow.

ISBN: 978-1-912364-60-2 (previously 978-1-908684-28-8)

Copyright © ElevenPlusExams.co.uk 2013

Second edition

All rights reserved. No part of this publication may be reproduced, stored or introduced into a retrieval system or transmitted in any form or by any means, without the prior written permission of the publisher nor may be circulated in any form of binding or cover other than the one in which it was published and without a similar condition including this condition being imposed on the subsequent publisher.

About Us

At Eleven Plus Exams, we supply high-quality 11 plus tuition for your children. Our free website at **www.elevenplusexams.co.uk** is the largest website in the UK that specifically prepares children for the 11 plus exams. We also provide online services to schools and our **First Past The Post®** range of books has been well-received by schools, tuition centres and parents.

Eleven Plus Exams is recognised as a trusted and authoritative source. We have been quoted in numerous national newspapers, including *The Telegraph*, *The Observer*, the *Daily Mail* and *The Sunday Telegraph*, as well as on national television (BBC1 and Channel 4), and BBC radio.

Our website offers a vast amount of information and advice on the 11 plus, including a moderated online forum, books, downloadable material and online services to enhance your child's chances of success. Set up in 2004, the website grew from an initial 20 webpages to more than 65,000 today, and has been visited by millions of parents. It is moderated by experts in the field, who provide support for parents both before and after the exams.

Don't forget to visit **www.elevenplusexams.co.uk** and see why we are the market's leading one-stop shop for all your 11 plus needs. You will find:

- ✓ Comprehensive quality content and advice written by 11 plus experts
- ✓ Eleven Plus Exams online shop supplying a wide range of practice books, e-papers, software and apps
- ✓ Lots of FREE practice papers to download
- ✓ Professional tuition service
- ✓ Short revision courses
- ✓ Year-long 11 plus courses
- ✓ Mock exams tailored to reflect those of the main examining bodies

Other Titles in the First Past The Post® Series
11+ Essentials Range of Books

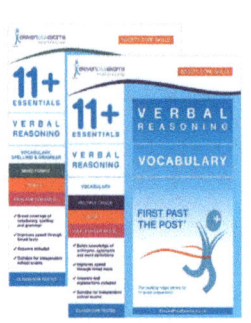

978-1-912364-60-2	Verbal Reasoning: Cloze Tests Book 1 - Mixed Format
978-1-912364-61-9	Verbal Reasoning: Cloze Tests Book 2 - Mixed Format
978-1-912364-78-7	Verbal Reasoning: Cloze Tests Book 3 - Mixed Format
978-1-912364-79-4	Verbal Reasoning: Cloze Tests Book 4 - Mixed Format
978-1-912364-62-6	Verbal Reasoning: Vocabulary Book 1 - Multiple Choice
978-1-912364-63-3	Verbal Reasoning: Vocabulary Book 2 - Multiple Choice
978-1-912364-64-0	Verbal Reasoning: Vocabulary Book 3 - Multiple Choice
978-1-912364-65-7	Verbal Reasoning: Vocabulary, Spelling and Grammar Book 1 - Multiple Choice
978-1-912364-66-4	Verbal Reasoning: Vocabulary, Spelling and Grammar Book 2 - Multiple Choice
978-1-912364-68-8	Verbal Reasoning: Vocabulary in Context Level 1
978-1-912364-69-5	Verbal Reasoning: Vocabulary in Context Level 2
978-1-912364-70-1	Verbal Reasoning: Vocabulary in Context Level 3
978-1-912364-71-8	Verbal Reasoning: Vocabulary in Context Level 4
978-1-912364-74-9	Verbal Reasoning: Vocabulary Puzzles Book 1
978-1-912364-75-6	Verbal Reasoning: Vocabulary Puzzles Book 2
978-1-912364-76-3	Verbal Reasoning: Practice Papers Book 1 - Multiple Choice
978-1-912364-77-0	Verbal Reasoning: Practice Papers Book 2 - Multiple Choice

978-1-912364-02-2	English: Comprehensions Classic Literature Book 1 - Multiple Choice
978-1-912364-03-9	English: Comprehensions Classic Literature Book 2 - Multiple Choice
978-1-912364-05-3	English: Comprehensions Contemporary Literature Book 1 - Multiple Choice
978-1-912364-06-0	English: Comprehensions Contemporary Literature Book 2 - Multiple Choice
978-1-912364-08-4	English: Comprehensions Non-Fiction Book 1 - Multiple Choice
978-1-912364-09-1	English: Comprehensions Non-Fiction Book 2 - Multiple Choice
978-1-912364-23-7	English: Comprehensions Poetry Book 1 - Multiple Choice
978-1-912364-14-5	English: Mini Comprehensions - Inference Book 1
978-1-912364-15-2	English: Mini Comprehensions - Inference Book 2
978-1-912364-16-9	English: Mini Comprehensions - Inference Book 3
978-1-912364-11-4	English: Mini Comprehensions - Fact-Finding Book 1
978-1-912364-12-1	English: Mini Comprehensions - Fact-Finding Book 2
978-1-912364-21-3	English: Spelling, Punctuation and Grammar Book 1
978-1-912364-22-0	English: Spelling, Punctuation and Grammar Book 2
978-1-912364-00-8	English: Practice Papers Book 1 - Multiple Choice
978-1-912364-01-5	English: Practice Papers Book 2 - Multiple Choice
978-1-912364-17-6	Creative Writing Examples 1
978-1-912364-24-4	Creative Writing Examples 2

978-1-912364-30-5	Numerical Reasoning: Quick-Fire Book 1
978-1-912364-31-2	Numerical Reasoning: Quick-Fire Book 2
978-1-912364-32-9	Numerical Reasoning: Quick-Fire Book 1 - Multiple Choice
978-1-912364-33-6	Numerical Reasoning: Quick-Fire Book 2 - Multiple Choice
978-1-912364-34-3	Numerical Reasoning: Multi-Part Book 1
978-1-912364-35-0	Numerical Reasoning: Multi-Part Book 2
978-1-912364-36-7	Numerical Reasoning: Multi-Part Book 1 - Multiple Choice
978-1-912364-37-4	Numerical Reasoning: Multi-Part Book 2 - Multiple Choice

978-1-912364-43-5	Mathematics: Mental Arithmetic Book 1
978-1-912364-44-2	Mathematics: Mental Arithmetic Book 2
978-1-912364-45-9	Mathematics: Worded Problems Book 1
978-1-912364-46-6	Mathematics: Worded Problems Book 2
978-1-912364-52-7	Mathematics: Worded Problems Book 3
978-1-912364-47-3	Mathematics: Dictionary Plus
978-1-912364-50-3	Mathematics: Crossword Puzzles Book 1
978-1-912364-51-0	Mathematics: Crossword Puzzles Book 2
978-1-912364-48-0	Mathematics: Practice Papers Book 1 - Multiple Choice
978-1-912364-49-7	Mathematics: Practice Papers Book 2 - Multiple Choice

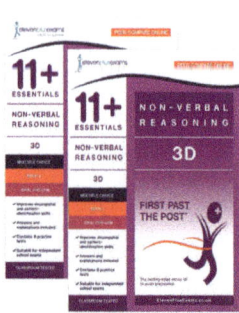

978-1-912364-87-9	Non-Verbal Reasoning: 2D Book 1 - Multiple Choice
978-1-912364-88-6	Non-Verbal Reasoning: 2D Book 2 - Multiple Choice
978-1-912364-85-5	Non-Verbal Reasoning: 3D Book 1 - Multiple Choice
978-1-912364-86-2	Non-Verbal Reasoning: 3D Book 2 - Multiple Choice
978-1-912364-83-1	Non-Verbal Reasoning: Practice Papers Book 1 - Multiple Choice

Contents

Word Bank

Test 1	The Altercation & Sharks	2
Test 2	The Moon & Phobias	4
Test 3	The Amazon River & Gateway of India	6
Test 4	The Great Wall of China	8
Test 5	The Inuit	10
Test 6	Florence Nightingale	11

Multiple Choice

Test 1	Benjamin Franklin & Volcanoes	16
Test 2	Earthquakes & The Black Death	18
Test 3	Alexander Graham Bell & Thomas Edison	20
Test 4	Ancient Rome	22
Test 5	The Human Brain	24
Test 6	St Paul's Cathedral	26

Partial Words

Test 1	Fossils & Baboons	32
Test 2	The Solar System & Piranhas	34
Test 3	Vikings & Morse Code	36
Test 4	The Ancient Olympic Games	38
Test 5	Braille	40
Test 6	Mount Everest	42

Answers   45

Peer-Compare access code   inside front cover

BLANK PAGE

Word Bank

Test 1

Total /24

6 minutes

Word Bank

| adventure | home | cacophony | altercation | emerged | talkative |
| escalated | longing | abhorrent | recent | trepidation | solitude |

The Altercation

The subdued man (1)_____ from the station relatively unscathed and immensely relieved to

be away from the (2)_____ crowd. He was somewhat bewildered at how a minor

(3)_____ on the train had swiftly (4)_____ into a barrage of obnoxious insults

towards him.

He was neither (5)_____ nor confident by nature, preferring the (6)_____ of his

own company, so the petrifying incident had left him (7)_____ for the familiarity and

tranquillity of his own (8)_____. The constant (9)_____ of the city no longer

enthralled him, and the (10)_____ confrontation only served to increase his feelings of

melancholy and (11)_____. That was when he knew his short-lived (12)_____

was over.

Test 1 (continued)

Word Bank					
seldom	efficient	enables	murky	acute	maintain
equipped	malicious	enormous	refined	cartilage	bulky

Sharks

Sharks are a type of fish, but, unlike other fish, they have (13)_____ instead of bone, which is

lighter and (14)_____ them to swim faster. One of the most (15)_____ sharks is

the great white shark, although it (16)_____ attacks people. Despite being

(17)_____ creatures, sometimes weighing over 20 tonnes, sharks do not sink as their livers

are well (18)_____ to hold a lot of oil, which helps them float and

(19)_____ buoyancy in the water.

Sharks are highly (20)_____ predators and have an (21)_____ sense of smell,

hearing and sight.

So (22)_____ are their senses that, in the water, they are able to smell their prey from

(23)_____ distances, and their eyes can see clearly even in the (24)_____

light of the ocean's depths.

Test 2

Total /16

4 minutes

Word Bank

collided	minute	waves	atmosphere	debris	Gravity
Earth					

The Moon

Scientists think that the Moon was formed 4.6 billion years ago from the (1)_____ that was

left over when a rock the size of Mars (2)_____ into the Earth.

The Moon has virtually no (3)_____, so no sound can be heard on its surface. This is because

sound waves bounce off (4)_____ particles in the atmosphere, called atoms, so with no

atmosphere, sound (5)_____ cannot travel.

The strength of (6)_____ on the Moon is approximately one-sixth of its strength here on the

Earth. The space suits worn by astronauts weigh 80 kilogrammes on (7)_____ but only 13

kilogrammes on the Moon.

Test 2 (continued)

Word Bank					
acquired	arachnophobia	irrational	phobia	heightened	specific
anxiety	agitated	bizarre			

Phobias

A phobia is an (8)_____ fear that a person feels when faced with a particular object or when in a (9)_____ situation. Approximately one in ten people suffer from a (10)_____, many of which are likely to have been (11)_____ during childhood.

Common phobias include a (12)_____ fear of spiders which is also known as (13)_____, fear of heights (acrophobia) and fear of dogs (cynophobia). Phobias that are more (14)_____ include fear of mirrors (catoptrophobia), fear of washing or cleaning (ablutophobia) and fear of sleep (hypnophobia).

People who have severe phobias often feel immense (15)_____ and consciously avoid situations they know will make them feel (16)_____, panicky and, in extreme cases, nauseous.

Test 3

Total /26

 6 minutes

Word Bank

responsible	species	river	shallow	longest	equivalent
impressive	tributaries	oceans	length	savage	second
snake	gallons				

The Amazon River

Located in South America, the colossal Amazon River is 4,000 miles long and is the second

(1)_____ river in the world, after the River Nile. It is also considered the broadest

(2)_____, carrying more water than the Mississippi, Nile and Yangtze rivers combined. It is

(3)_____ for about one-fifth of the freshwater that flows into the world's

(4)_____. There are no bridges across the entire (5)_____ of the river. The

(6)_____ Amazon has more than 1,000 (7)_____, streams or smaller rivers that

flow into a main river. The river is inhabited by thousands of (8)_____ of plants, animals and

fish, including the (9)_____ piranha and the anaconda (10)_____, which is found

in the (11)_____ waters of the river. The Amazon pours 60 million

(12)_____ of water into the Atlantic Ocean every (13)_____, and the amount of

water that flows through it each day is (14)_____ to the total amount of water used in New

York City over 12 years.

Test 3 (continued)

Word Bank					
commence	heralded	country	British	emperor	independence
commemorate	visited	waterfront	ceremonial	monument	construction

Gateway of India

The Gateway of India is a huge stone **(15)**_____ built by the Indian government to

(16)_____ the landing of King George V, **(17)**_____ of India during British rule,

and his wife Queen Mary, when they **(18)**_____ India in 1911.

However, they only managed to see a cardboard model of the edifice, since **(19)**_____ of the

monument did not **(20)**_____ until 1915, and it was not completed until 1924.

Designed by Scotsman George Wittet and located on the Mumbai **(21)**_____ overlooking the

Arabian Sea, the Gateway of India became the **(22)**_____ entrance to India for Viceroys and

the new Governors of Mumbai. It was **(23)**_____ as a symbol of the power of the British

Empire.

Following India's **(24)**_____, which signalled the end of British rule, the last

(25)_____ troops left the **(26)**_____ passing through the gateway in a ceremony

in 1948.

Test 4

Total /20

5 minutes

Word Bank

perception	conscripted	architecture	edifice	network	Dynasty
continuous	cemetery	plateaus	laborious	resplendent	importance
scenery	world	disgraced	enhanced	sections	construction
emperors	heritage				

The Great Wall of China

China is a land of beautiful **(1)**_____ and ancient temples, with thousands of years of rich

cultural **(2)**_____. It is also home to the longest man-made structure in the

(3)_____, the Great Wall of China.

Built over a period of 2,000 years, the **(4)**_____ structure spans approximately 4,000 miles

across China's deserts, mountains and **(5)**_____.

Contrary to many people's **(6)**_____ of the Great Wall being one **(7)**_____

structure, it is in fact a **(8)**_____ of many individual wall segments, which were built at

various times and commissioned by multiple **(9)**_____ to protect the Chinese empire from its enemies.

Although work began as early as 221 BC under the first emperor of China, many (10)_____ of the wall have since been rebuilt and (11)_____. The majority of the existing wall was reconstructed during the Ming (12)_____ from 1368 to 1644.

Building the wall was a challenging and (13)_____ task, often undertaken in unbearable working conditions by more than 300,000 prisoners, peasants and (14)_____ noblemen.

Not only did they have to endure backbreaking work, they were (15)_____ to leave their families for several years at a time to construct the (16)_____.

Working on the wall was so hazardous that, during its (17)_____, the Great Wall was referred to as 'the longest (18)_____ on Earth', because more than one million people lost their lives building it. So appealing is its (19)_____ and historical (20)_____, that the Great Wall attracts as many as 10 million visitors each year.

Test 5

Total /17

 4 minutes

Word Bank

region	integral	winter	nourishment	solely	ice
frozen	sledges	paramount	survive	environment	hostile
relationship	meat	diet	prey	inhabited	

The Inuit

The Arctic area of North America is one of the most remote and (1)_____ places on Earth.

Despite this, it is (2)_____ by four million Inuit people. During the bleak

(3)_____ months, the entire (4)_____ is frozen, and the Inuit are forced to

(5)_____ in sub-zero temperatures with no daylight. Their survival in such conditions is

(6)_____ dependent on their vast knowledge and understanding of their

(7)_____. Hunting and fishing is of (8)_____ importance to the Inuit people and

is their only means of (9)_____. Their (10)_____ consists of whale, walrus,

moose and seal (11)_____, which they hunt by waiting at air holes the seals make in the

(12)_____. Their (13)_____ with animals is not limited to that of hunter and

(14)_____; dogs are an (15)_____ part of their lives and are relied on to pull

(16)_____ across many miles of (17)_____ sea.

Test 6

Total /29

 8 minutes

Word Bank

unsanitary	recuperation	campaign	inventing	destitute	elected
vocation	humanitarian	fortunate	procedures	destiny	mortality
wounded	nature	hospitals	heroine	earning	profound
arrangement	regard	influential	nursing	significant	located
training	desires	era	statistician	profession	

Florence Nightingale

Florence Nightingale was born in 1820 and was a celebrated social reformer and **(1)**_____.

Although raised in a period where women's sole occupation was to marry well and bear children,

Florence always believed that her **(2)**_____ lay in something greater. Her profound religious

faith instilled a strong moral duty to help the less **(3)**_____.

Against the **(4)**_____ of her parents, her belief in God led to a growing conviction that

nursing was to be her **(5)**_____. Florence's parents eventually relented and gave their

permission for her to undertake three months **(6)**_____ training at a hospital in Germany.

She is most acclaimed for serving as a nurse and tending to **(7)**_____ soldiers during the

Crimean War. Cholera and malaria were rife among the British soldiers **(8)**_____ in army

hospitals in Turkey, where Florence volunteered her services. Upon her arrival, she was appalled at the

(9)_____ and harsh conditions that contributed to the high (10)_____ rate

amongst the wounded and disease-ridden soldiers.

Florence thus embarked on a mission to reorganise the (11)_____ and improve supplies of

blankets, beds and food, as well as raise the standard of cleanliness. Her benevolent

(12)_____ knew no bounds, and she often checked on the soldiers during the night with the

aid of a lamp, (13)_____ her the name 'Lady with the Lamp'.

Upon her return to Britain, Florence was deemed a (14)_____ for her extraordinary efforts

and revolutionary thinking. Furthermore, her insightful reforms and ideas have had a

(15)_____ influence on the nature of modern healthcare, and her tireless

(16)_____ to improve health standards and hospital planning continue to be held in high

(17)_____.

Prior to Florence's (18)_____ efforts in the field of nursing, the profession held negative

connotations and was considered appropriate only for (19)_____ women. However, through

her noble efforts, she successfully transformed nursing into an honourable (20)_____ for

women and, in 1860, was instrumental in establishing the first professional (21)_____ school for nurses.

Florence's influence on nursing is still evident today, particularly in the (22)_____ of hospital wards, which are based on her finding that the organisation of a hospital has a (23)_____ impact on the health and recovery of its patients. Moreover, the introduction of her pioneering (24)_____, combined with a healthy diet, continues to be recognised as a key factor in assisting the (25)_____ process.

Among Florence's numerous achievements, she is credited with (26)_____ the pie chart, and subsequently became the first woman to be (27)_____ to the Royal Statistical Society, a position typically reserved for men during this (28)_____.

Florence died in 1910 at the age of 90, but not before becoming one of the most (29)_____ and famous women of the 19th century.

BLANK PAGE

Multiple Choice

Test 1

Total /17

4 minutes

Benjamin Franklin

Born in 1706, Benjamin Franklin was one of the **(1)** ☐ Founding ☐ Foundling ☐ Foundered Fathers of the United States of

America and played a **(2)** ☐ pivotal ☐ gratuitous ☐ pivoted role in America's struggle for independence.

An extremely **(3)** ☐ amateurish ☐ unaccomplished ☐ versatile man, Franklin was also a **(4)** ☐ cerebral ☐ celebrated ☐ undiscovered politician,

writer, scientist and inventor, who **(5)** ☐ frequented ☐ frequently ☐ frequency used his home as a laboratory for conducting

electrical experiments. To this day, he is greatly admired for his **(6)** ☐ discoveries ☐ desires ☐ desperation and theories

regarding **(7)** ☐ gas. ☐ electricity. ☐ biology.

One of his most **(8)** ☐ prominent ☐ primed ☐ medieval inventions was the lightning rod, **(9)** ☐ designated ☐ designed ☐ desiccated to protect

buildings from catching **(10)** ☐ fire ☐ currents ☐ currants during electrical storms. This invention earned Franklin

(11) ☐ region ☐ worldwide ☐ marginal fame and respect and is still used to protect **(12)** ☐ arenas ☐ towns ☐ buildings across the globe.

© 2013 ElevenPlusExams.co.uk   COPYING STRICTLY PROHIBITED

Test 1 (continued)

Volcanoes

Volcanoes are **(13)** ☐ cavalries / ☐ cavities / ☐ caves in the surface of the Earth. Occasionally, a build-up of **(14)** ☐ fissure / ☐ pressured / ☐ pressure causes the volcano to erupt **(15)** ☐ bashfully, / ☐ forcefully, / ☐ gracefully, blasting out hot ash, gas and lava. Sometimes, so **(16)** ☐ vigorous / ☐ vigilant / ☐ vicarious is the blast that it can send ash soaring as high as 17 miles into the air. The hot, red lava flows down the side of the volcano and **(17)** ☐ solidifies / ☐ fragments / ☐ ferments as it cools down.

Test 2

Total /18

4 minutes

Earthquakes

The **(1)** ☐ superficial ☐ peripheral ☐ saturated surface of the Earth is made up of several **(2)** ☐ colossal ☐ infinitesimal ☐ malleable slabs of rock called tectonic plates, which are **(3)** ☐ accurately ☐ perpetually ☐ pompously shifting. The line along which two plates meet, and sometimes **(4)** ☐ disconnect ☐ conjoin ☐ concur is known as a fault line. Here, immense pressure builds up, until a **(5)** ☐ vigorous ☐ insubstantial ☐ wavering release of energy occurs at what is known as the epicentre of an earthquake. This is the point from which rocks **(6)** ☐ absorb ☐ emit ☐ ooze waves of energy. The waves then travel up to the Earth's surface where tremors are felt. Modern technology has led it to **(7)** ☐ transpire ☐ erupt ☐ disappear that thousands of earthquakes occur around the globe every year, but most are too weak to be detected and occur in remote and **(8)** ☐ inaccessible ☐ inconvenient ☐ inconceivable locations.

Test 2 (continued)

The Black Death

The Black Death was a lethal **(9)** [ ] pandemic / [ ] distraction / [ ] illnesses that ravaged Europe between 1347 and 1351. So **(10)** [ ] insignificant / [ ] trivial / [ ] virulent was the disease that it claimed the lives of more than 75 million people globally, more than any other known **(11)** [ ] moment / [ ] illness / [ ] catastrophic at that time. The outbreak was made more severe by the **(12)** [ ] squalid / [ ] hygienic / [ ] sanitary conditions that most people endured in medieval European cities. Many health problems were **(13)** [ ] innocuous / [ ] associated / [ ] haphazard with overcrowding and **(14)** [ ] primitive / [ ] technological / [ ] modern sanitation and sewage systems, so transmission through the European **(15)** [ ] population / [ ] local / [ ] resident was inevitable. Many people believed the **(16)** [ ] plague / [ ] ravage / [ ] destroy was a punishment for their sins, and, to **(17)** [ ] inflame / [ ] alleviate / [ ] exacerbate the wrath of God, they engaged in acts of **(18)** [ ] penitence / [ ] petulance / [ ] retribution in the hope that they would be spared.

Test 3

Total /19

 4 minutes

Alexander Graham Bell

Alexander Graham Bell was an **(1)** ☐ obscure ☐ ambiguous ☐ illustrious scientist and teacher of the deaf, but he is most

(2) ☐ celebrated ☐ calibrated ☐ infamous for inventing the telephone in 1876. He was born in Scotland in 1847 and, over

many years of his life, developed a **(3)** ☐ transient ☐ ephemeral ☐ profound fascination with the idea of transmitting speech.

It was whilst working at a school for deaf children that Bell fashioned a **(4)** ☐ device ☐ artefact ☐ code which could

transmit the human voice via an electric **(5)** ☐ beam; ☐ currant; ☐ current; this came to be known as the telephone.

His invention was an **(6)** ☐ astronomical ☐ astrological ☐ meteoric success and financially very **(7)** ☐ profitable, ☐ absorptive, ☐ prescriptive, which

meant he was able to spend time on other inventions, including **(8)** ☐ horseshoes ☐ hydrofoils ☐ hieroglyphics and the metal

detector. Bell died in 1922, but not without leaving a lasting **(9)** ☐ fallacy ☐ legacy ☐ autocracy for the world to enjoy.

Test 3 (continued)

Thomas Edison

Thomas Edison was born in 1847 and was **(10)** ☐ irresponsibly ☐ irregularly ☐ undeniably one of the greatest inventors and

(11) ☐ peers ☐ scrutineers ☐ pioneers of the 19th century.

He is credited with a **(12)** ☐ scarcity ☐ multitude ☐ paucity of inventions, all of which have had a significant

(13) ☐ affluence ☐ impact ☐ interference on people's lives around the world. These include, amongst others, the electric

motor, the **(14)** ☐ motion ☐ motionless ☐ motivation picture, the phonograph and the **(15)** ☐ affable ☐ affordable ☐ affluent electric light.

Edison's **(16)** ☐ apathy ☐ inquisitiveness ☐ empathy was sparked at an early age, and he was encouraged by his parents

to pursue his **(17)** ☐ ardent ☐ denial ☐ idle passion for invention.

By the time he died in 1931, he had **(18)** ☐ patterned ☐ patented ☐ painted 1,092 devices, making him the most

(19) ☐ prolific ☐ prophetic ☐ unbecoming inventor in history.

Test 4

Total /16

 4 minutes

Ancient Rome

Ancient Rome was a (1) ☐ declining / ☐ contemporary / ☐ flourishing civilisation that began growing on the Italian Peninsula at

the beginning of the 8th (2) ☐ centenary / ☐ centuries / ☐ century BC. Gradually, the Roman Empire expanded to

(3) ☐ eliminate / ☐ encompass / ☐ encroach most of Western Europe, Western Asia, Northern Africa and the Mediterranean

islands. At the height of its (4) ☐ sovereignty / ☐ sovereign / ☐ transience around 150 AD, Rome controlled the greatest

(5) ☐ empire / ☐ country / ☐ nation ever seen in Europe.

Many of the (6) ☐ liberated / ☐ conquered / ☐ beleaguered nations benefited under Roman rule as the (7) ☐ disadvantaged / ☐ undeveloped / ☐ advanced

road system they established enabled (8) ☐ unrestricted / ☐ restricted / ☐ partial trade throughout the Empire, increasing

access to (9) ☐ capacious / ☐ copious / ☐ Capricorn amounts of affordable goods. Subsequently, most conquered societies enjoyed greater (10) ☐ intensity / ☐ prosperity / ☐ destitution under Roman rule, which offered them a better way of

(11) ☐ eating. / ☐ life. / ☐ dressing.

Religion was of (12) ☐ minimal / ☐ paramount / ☐ paltry importance to the Romans, who held the belief that the gods

(13) ☐ controlled / ☐ disciplined / ☐ christened their lives, and explanations of most events (14) ☐ typically / ☐ infrequently / ☐ typologically invoked

divine intervention. They spent vast amounts of time worshipping (15) ☐ people, / ☐ nature, / ☐ deities, both at home and

in the numerous (16) ☐ temples / ☐ cenotaphs / ☐ monumental which were built throughout the Empire.

Test 5

Total /19

5 minutes

The Human Brain

Humans have the largest brain relative to body size of all animals. It weighs **(1)**
- [ ] appreciative
- [ ] approximately
- [ ] admiringly

1.5kg and is one of the most **(2)**
- [ ] intricate
- [ ] intrepid
- [ ] interim

parts of the human body, so much so that scientists still

(3)
- [ ] devour
- [ ] endeavour
- [ ] ignored

to understand it.

It is consists of about 75 percent water and is the most energy-demanding of all the **(4)**
- [ ] organisms
- [ ] organs
- [ ] limbs

in our body. The brain comprises several **(5)**
- [ ] companies
- [ ] components
- [ ] companions

and, along with the spinal cord, makes up the central **(6)**
- [ ] circulatory
- [ ] digestive
- [ ] nervous

system, controlling everything from our thoughts and memories to our decisions and movements.

The cerebrum is the largest of the four **(7)**
- [ ] principle
- [ ] population
- [ ] principal

sections of the brain, constituting up to 85 percent of the brain's total **(8)**
- [ ] impasse,
- [ ] muse,
- [ ] mass,

and is associated with higher brain **(9)**
- [ ] production.
- [ ] function.
- [ ] functional.

It is in this part of the brain where perception, **(10)**
- [ ] image,
- [ ] imaginably,
- [ ] imagination,

thought, judgement and

decisions occur.

Our brains are **(11)** ☐ complex / ☐ informative / ☐ controversial   and can do incredible things to help us

(12) ☐ navigate / ☐ circumnavigate / ☐ conjugate   our busy lives and make sense of the world.

For instance, when you sleep, your brain produces a **(13)** ☐ cyclone / ☐ velodrome / ☐ hormone   that paralyses you to

(14) ☐ premise / ☐ prevent / ☐ persuade   you from acting out your dreams.

In addition, while you are awake, your brain **(15)** ☐ generates / ☐ thwarts / ☐ obstructs   between 11 and 23 watts of power;

that is enough energy to **(16)** ☐ illuminate / ☐ disable / ☐ produce   a light bulb!

Although the brain stops growing when you reach 18, **(17)** ☐ recalling / ☐ recanting / ☐ recasting   memories or information

helps you create new **(18)** ☐ connections / ☐ concoctions / ☐ enzymes   in your brain whatever age you are.

Creating new connections in the brain **(19)** ☐ entices / ☐ encircles / ☐ enhances   your ability to process and remember

information.

Test 6

Total /40

9 minutes

St Paul's Cathedral

With its majestic dome, St Paul's Cathedral is one of London's most **(1)** ☐ apprehensive ☐ recognisable ☐ approachable sights. It

has **(2)** ☐ dominated ☐ sullied ☐ tainted the city's skyline for over 300 years. However, throughout history, the

(3) ☐ conventional ☐ prosaic ☐ resplendent cathedral has been **(4)** ☐ beguiled ☐ plagued ☐ charmed by grave misfortune, and it has had to

be **(5)** ☐ instructed ☐ broken ☐ reconstructed on numerous occasions.

The initial building was created in the year 604 but was tragically **(6)** ☐ dissolved ☐ engraved ☐ engulfed by a fire during a

Viking **(7)** ☐ inquest ☐ invasion ☐ invitation of 962. Construction of a Gothic-style **(8)** ☐ cathedral ☐ pens ☐ sanctuary commenced in

1087, following the Norman Conquest. Once again, another **(9)** ☐ advantageous ☐ calamitous ☐ constructive fire in 1136 caused

significant delays, and it was not for another 200 years that the **(10)** ☐ edifice ☐ orifice ☐ edible was finally completed

in 1310.

Known as Old St Paul's, the cathedral was an enormous (11) ☐ disappointing / ☐ accomplishment / ☐ accompaniment   at that time and

was (12) ☐ purported / ☐ threatened / ☐ forbidden   to be the largest medieval building in Europe. It was

(13) ☐ eligible / ☐ excluded / ☐ alleged   to have the world's tallest (14) ☐ sapphire / ☐ spire / ☐ sphere   and some of the finest stained

glass windows. (15) ☐ Monarchs / ☐ Nomads / ☐ Mobsters   and noblemen often attended Mass, the official

(16) ☐ censorship / ☐ apprenticeship / ☐ worship   service of Catholicism, and court business was sometimes

(17) ☐ conducted / ☐ convoluted / ☐ cancelled   in the church. Old St Paul's stood tall and (18) ☐ yielding / ☐ unyielding / ☐ pliable   until several

centuries later, suffering from wear and tear, it began crumbling into a state of (19) ☐ impeccability. / ☐ depression. / ☐ dilapidation.

Further tragedy (20) ☐ exaggerated / ☐ besieged / ☐ benefitted   the cathedral in 1561, when the spire burned down after being

struck by (21) ☐ hail. / ☐ lightning. / ☐ lighting.   It was during this time that the (22) ☐ lackadaisical / ☐ indifferent / ☐ distinguished   architect,

Sir Christopher Wren, recommended the tower be taken down and replaced with a classical

(23) ☐ domain, ☐ dome, ☐ sphere, a design inspired by Parisian church (24) ☐ architecture, ☐ archaeologists, ☐ librarians, which was greatly admired by Wren.

However, before the project had even begun, it had to be abandoned as another (25) ☐ apostrophe ☐ catastrophe ☐ cacophony occurred in 1667 when the Great Fire of London (26) ☐ covered ☐ ravaged ☐ swayed the narrow streets, reducing St Paul's to (27) ☐ charred ☐ branded ☐ churlish timbers and ash. In the (28) ☐ immersion ☐ aftermath ☐ cohesion of the raging inferno, Wren was (29) ☐ commissioned ☐ commiserated ☐ commemorated to build a new cathedral in 1675.

In comparison to previous (30) ☐ medieval ☐ Tudor ☐ Roman cathedrals, which took centuries to construct, Wren's (31) ☐ mastication ☐ personification ☐ masterpiece was completed in just 35 years and was the most (32) ☐ mediocre ☐ trifling ☐ prodigious building project of that time. Featuring baroque designs and a (33) ☐ prominent ☐ darken ☐ problematic dome, the awe-inspiring cathedral that stands today is a result of Wren's (34) ☐ charisma ☐ ingenious ☐ gracious artistic vision and one that **(35)** ☐ occupies ☐ preoccupies ☐ defies a significant place in London's history.

On his death in 1723, Wren was buried in St Paul's Cathedral, and a Latin **(36)** ☐ prescription ☐ inscription ☐ conscription near his tomb **(37)** ☐ infers ☐ translates ☐ transcends as 'Reader, if you seek his monument, look around you.'

Other **(38)** ☐ notable ☐ frivolous ☐ inconsequential figures buried in the **(39)** ☐ alcoves ☐ belfry ☐ crypts of St Paul's Cathedral include the **(40)** ☐ ghastly ☐ military ☐ loathed heroes Lord Nelson and the Duke of Wellington.

BLANK PAGE

Cloze Tests

PARTIAL WORDS

Test 1

Total /17

5 minutes

Fossils

Fossils are the preserved remains or **(1)** ☐mpre☐s☐ons of long-dead organisms. They provide

evidence of the life that existed on Earth millions of years ago. They are studied by

(2) p☐lae☐ntol☐gi☐t☐ and other scientists to learn about the types of plants,

(3) ☐nim☐l☐ , and other organisms which used to exist, and they can tell us a lot about

(4) ev☐lut☐on. Although fossils can be found in many places, such as on beaches and in

(5) qua☐rie☐, in most cases, they are discovered by exhuming layers of **(6)** sed☐men☐ary

rock formed of silt, sand and mud which has **(7)** s☐lid☐fie☐ over time. It is as these rocks get

eroded by forces of nature, such as wind and water, that the fossils inside are **(8)** r☐v☐ale☐.

Test 1 (continued)

Baboons

The baboon is one of the most **(9) pr⬜val⬜nt** species of monkey in Africa and, despite

(10) d⬜scern⬜b⬜e differences from us, they are closely related to humans. They live in large

(11) p⬜triar⬜hal troops of 20 to a few hundred members. These consist of females, their offspring

and several resident and **(12) tra⬜s⬜ent** males, some of whom leave and change troops every few

years. Baboons are often wrongly considered to be dangerous and **(13) ⬜indic⬜iv⬜**. However,

their relationships are worked out in a **(14) r⬜cipr⬜cal** system. Baboons are **(15) terr⬜stri⬜l**

and spend most of their time on the ground, where they must be **(16) v⬜gil⬜n⬜** of predators.

Their diets are mostly **(17) he⬜biv⬜rou⬜**, but they also eat insects, fish, birds and mammals.

Test 2

Total /23

6 minutes

The Solar System

(1) S☐ie☐ti☐ts think that the Solar System is 4.6 (2) b☐☐☐i☐n years old. Our

(3) ☐ol☐r System comprises eight planets which (4) ☐r☐it the Sun. It also has many

(5) sm☐☐le☐ bodies, such as comets, moons and (6) m☐t☐oro☐d☐ and plenty of

dust and gas. The largest planet is (7) ☐u☐it☐r, named after the Roman god of the same name.

It is known to be the most (8) t☐rbu☐en☐ planet in the Solar System. This is because it

(9) ☐pin☐ faster than any other planet, creating an ever-changing (10) wh☐rlp☐o☐ of

storms. The third planet from the Sun, known as the Blue Planet, is (11) ☐☐rth, and it lies 150

million kilometres away from the Sun.

Test 2 (continued)

Piranhas

Piranhas are **(12)** f☐esh☐ate☐ fish that inhabit South American **(13)** ☐iv☐rs. They are covered in scales that reflect sunlight and provide **(14)** c☐mo☐fl☐ge, preventing them from being spotted by **(15)** p☐edat☐☐s above the water's surface. Their **(16)** p☐we☐fu☐ jaws and razor-sharp teeth have earned piranhas a **(17)** r☐pu☐ati☐n as blood thirsty, **(18)** f☐r☐ci☐u☐ creatures who launch **(19)** f☐enz☐e☐ attacks on large animals.

However, the reality is that the **(20)** ☐i☐anh☐ is a timid **(21)** sc☐v☐n☐e☐ with an appetite for insects, fish, fruits, seeds, birds, **(22)** aq☐at☐c plants and lizards. Generally, piranhas are of little threat to **(23)** ☐um☐n☐, and it is rare for them to attack people.

Test 3

Total /18

5 minutes

Vikings

The Vikings **(1) h☐ile☐** from Scandinavia, a region which consists of modern-day Denmark, Sweden, Norway, and Finland. They left their land in search of abundance and **(2) a☐☐e☐t☐re**. This period in **(3) h☐st☐☐y** was known as the Viking Age. It began in the late 8th century and lasted for about 300 years. Vikings were a **(4) se☐far☐ng** people who explored, invaded and **(5) s☐tt☐e☐** in areas of Europe, Asia and the North Atlantic islands. Although they are widely known for their savage and **(6) f☐ars☐m☐** raids of other lands, many of them were adept farmers and **(7) pr☐l☐fi☐** craftsmen, who were capable of building large ships from **(8) p☐a☐k☐** of timber.

Test 3 (continued)

Morse Code

Morse code is a means of **(9) tr☐☐smit☐in☐** messages in which letters of the alphabet are

represented by a **(10) c☐mbi☐atio☐** of long and short electrical **(11) p☐lse☐**, flashes of

light or sounds. Invented by Samuel Morse in the 1840s, it was initially used to send

(12) ☐☐fo☐m☐ti☐n over a long-distance electrical **(13) ☐om☐un☐cat☐☐n**

system called telegraphy. The most **(14) r☐cog☐☐s☐d** Morse code phrase is the

(15) di☐tr☐s☐ signal 'SOS', which is often thought to stand for 'Save Our Souls'. Morse code is

still used today by **(16) ☐m☐t☐ur** radio operators and by the **(17) Na☐☐** for conveying

messages between **(18) n☐v☐l** ships.

Test 4

Total /18

5 minutes

The Ancient Olympic Games

The first **(1)** ☐ly☐p☐☐ Games were part of a religious **(2)** f☐☐t☐va☐ held more

than 2,700 years ago in Olympia in **(3)** Gr☐☐☐☐. They were known as the Greek Olympics and

were **(4)** ded☐c☐t☐d to the Greek God Zeus. Before the **(5)** ☐☐me☐ began, any wars

in progress had to stop for one **(6)** ☐o☐th so that the participants could get to the **(7)** ☐i☐y

of the Games safely. Each city would pay for a few **(8)** at☐l☐tes to travel to the event, but there

were many **(9)** r☐le☐ that had to be followed. All competitors had to **(10)** p☐☐mis☐ that

they had trained for at least **(11)** ☐☐n months. As this **(12)** m☐an☐ that they would need to take time off work to train, only **(13) w☐al☐hy** men could take part.

At first, the Games only had one **(14) ☐ven☐**, a race from one end of the **(15) st☐d☐u☐** to the other covering 170 metres, but, over **(16) ☐im☐**, other events were added. These included wrestling, **(17) ☐ox☐n☐**, chariot racing and the long jump. However, unlike the **(18) m☐d☐r☐** Olympic Games, women were not allowed to take part or even watch!

Test 5

Total /28

7 minutes

Braille

Braille is a reading and **(1)** ▢rit▢ng system used by the blind or visually **(2)** imp▢ire▢ that

was developed by Louis Braille in 1809. At the age of three, Louis was involved in a

(3) c▢t▢▢t▢ophi▢ accident in which he accidentally **(4)** ▢ok▢d his eye with a

sharp tool and **(5)** ▢ubs▢q▢en▢ly lost his sight. When Louis grew older, he won a

(6) ▢ch▢l▢▢s▢▢p to the Royal Institution for Blind Youth in Paris. It was here that he

(7) e▢p▢r▢me▢te▢ with ways to create an alphabet that could be read with one's

(8) f▢nge▢t▢ps. In 1824, he **(9)** ▢nv▢nt▢d the Braille code. It was based on a

(10) ▢ys▢em called 'Night Writing', which **(11)** so▢di▢r▢ used to communicate with

one another during the night. Night Writing **(12)** c▢mpr▢s▢d lots of dots and

(13) d☐sh☐s, which Louis adapted to make each character a small, (14) r☐ct☐ngu☐a☐ block, which in turn contained (15) m☐nis☐ul☐ raised dots.

The (16) ☐rr☐ng☐m☐☐t and number of dots enable Braille readers to (17) di☐ti☐gu☐s☐ one character from another. Each cell can be used to (18) ☐epr☐s☐nt a letter of the alphabet, a (19) ☐unc☐u☐t☐☐n mark, a number or an entire (20) ☐or☐. Braille can be written in (21) ☐ume☐o☐s ways. Blind people can write using (22) sp☐c☐a☐ apparatus called a slate and stylus; they can also now use a Braille (23) ty☐ew☐ite☐ or a computer with (24) ☐r☐ill☐ translation software and a Braille embosser, a (25) sp☐c☐f☐c type of printer which leaves a (26) tan☐ib☐e Braille cell imprint on paper. Many years later, thanks to Louis' work and (27) ☐ed☐c☐ti☐n, millions of blind and (28) ☐isu☐l☐y impaired people around the world are able to read and write.

Test 6

Total /28

7 minutes

Mount Everest

With a **(1) so☐ri☐g** peak of 29,035 feet, Mount Everest is a place of **(2) u☐par☐ll☐led** beauty and is the highest mountain in the world. Situated along the border of Nepal, Tibet and China, its **(3) tr☐nscen☐ent** height reaches five and a half miles into the sky.

Everest forms part of the Himalayan mountain range which **(4) trav☐rs☐s** 1,500 miles across Asia.

The mountain is over 60 million years old and was formed by the **(5) c☐llisio☐** of the Indian tectonic plate pushing against the Eurasian plate with **(6) ☐ubst☐ntial** force. This **(7) ☐nst☐gat☐d** a build up of pressure between the plates, forcing the Earth's surface to push upwards. Even today, the plates continue to shift, and each year, Mount Everest grows a quarter of an inch higher. In 1865, it was named after Sir George Everest, the British surveyor general of India and the first person to **(8) d☐cum☐nt** its height and locality.

With **(9) f☐☐mid☐ble** winds blowing up to 200 miles per hour and sub-zero temperatures falling to below minus 40 degrees Celsius, Everest is an extremely inhospitable mountain and presents climbers with an **(10) a☐☐nd☐nce** of dangers. As well as freezing conditions which **(11) habi☐ual☐y** result in frostbite and hypothermia, avalanches are a constant **(12) h☐z☐rd**, and the shifting glaciers can **(13) precip☐tous☐y** create deep crevasses, of which climbers must be (14) v☐gi☐ant. However, one of the most challenging (15) p☐ril☐

the mountain poses is the (16) sc☐rci☐y of oxygen and the illnesses associated with this. At the

snow-capped peak of Everest, oxygen levels are only a third of what they are at sea level, and this can

have an (17) adv☐rs☐ effect on a person's breathing, heart rate, coordination, sleep, judgement

and balance. In some cases, (18) alt☐tud☐ sickness has proven to be fatal. Ascending the majestic

mountain is a (19) pr☐ca☐ious feat, and one that has claimed the lives of more than 200 people.

Between 1920 and 1952, there were (20) nume☐ou☐ attempts to reach its peak, but all were

unsuccessful, and in one case led to the (21) f☐te☐ul death of the famous mountaineer, George

Leigh-Mallory. The first people to conquer Everest and reach its (22) s☐mm☐t were Sir Edmund

Hilary and Tenzing Norgay on May 19th 1953. They formed part of the British (23) exp☐dit☐on

led by Colonel John Hunt, who had selected a team of eleven exceptionally (24) pr☐ficien☐

climbers from all around the British Empire. Upon reaching the mountaintop, they could see at least a

hundred miles in every direction and witnessed (25) g☐or☐☐us views of mountains, glaciers

and high (26) plat☐aus. More than six decades later, their historic (27) as☐ent remains to be

one of the 20th century's most (28) m☐ment☐us triumphs.

BLANK PAGE

FIRST PAST THE POST

Answers

Verbal Reasoning:

Cloze Tests

Mixed Format

Book 1

Cloze Tests: Word Bank

Test 1, pages 2-3

The Altercation

1	emerged
2	abhorrent
3	altercation
4	escalated
5	talkative
6	solitude
7	longing
8	home
9	cacophony
10	recent
11	trepidation
12	adventure

Sharks

13	cartilage
14	enables
15	malicious
16	seldom
17	bulky
18	equipped
19	maintain
20	efficient
21	acute
22	refined
23	enormous
24	murky

Test 2, pages 4-5

The Moon

1	debris
2	collided
3	atmosphere
4	minute
5	waves
6	Gravity
7	Earth

Phobias

8	irrational
9	specific
10	phobia
11	acquired
12	heightened
13	arachnophobia
14	bizarre
15	anxiety
16	agitated

Test 3, pages 6-7

The Amazon River

1	longest
2	river
3	responsible
4	oceans
5	length
6	impressive
7	tributaries
8	species
9	savage
10	snake
11	shallow
12	gallons
13	second
14	equivalent

Gateway of India

15	monument
16	commemorate
17	emperor
18	visited
19	construction
20	commence
21	waterfront
22	ceremonial
23	heralded
24	independence
25	British
26	country

Cloze Tests: Word Bank

Test 4, pages 8-9
The Great Wall of China

1	scenery
2	heritage
3	world
4	resplendent
5	plateaus
6	perception
7	continuous
8	network
9	emperors
10	sections
11	enhanced
12	Dynasty
13	laborious
14	disgraced
15	conscripted
16	edifice
17	construction
18	cemetery
19	architecture
20	importance

Test 5, page 10
The Inuit

1	hostile
2	inhabited
3	winter
4	region
5	survive
6	solely
7	environment
8	paramount
9	nourishment
10	diet
11	meat
12	ice
13	relationship
14	prey
15	integral
16	sledges
17	frozen

Test 6, pages 11-13
Florence Nightingale

1	statistician
2	destiny
3	fortunate
4	desires
5	vocation
6	nursing
7	wounded
8	located
9	unsanitary
10	mortality
11	hospitals
12	nature
13	earning
14	heroine
15	profound
16	campaign
17	regard
18	humanitarian
19	destitute
20	profession
21	training
22	arrangement
23	significant
24	procedures
25	recuperation
26	inventing
27	elected
28	era
29	influential

Cloze Tests: Multiple Choice

Test 1, pages 16-17

Benjamin Franklin

1	Founding
2	pivotal
3	versatile
4	celebrated
5	frequently
6	discoveries
7	electricity
8	prominent
9	designed
10	fire
11	worldwide
12	buildings

Volcanoes

13	cavities
14	pressure
15	forcefully
16	vigorous
17	solidifies

Test 2, pages 18-19

Earthquakes

1	peripheral
2	colossal
3	perpetually
4	conjoin
5	vigorous
6	emit
7	transpire
8	inaccessible

The Black Death

9	pandemic
10	virulent
11	illness
12	squalid
13	associated
14	primitive
15	population
16	plague
17	alleviate
18	penitence

Test 3, pages 20-21

Alexander Graham Bell

1	illustrious
2	celebrated
3	profound
4	device
5	current
6	astronomical
7	profitable
8	hydrofoils
9	legacy

Thomas Edison

10	undeniably
11	pioneers
12	multitude
13	impact
14	motion
15	affordable
16	inquisitiveness
17	ardent
18	patented
19	prolific

Cloze Tests: Multiple Choice

Test 4, pages 22-23
Ancient Rome

1	flourishing
2	century
3	encompass
4	sovereignty
5	empire
6	conquered
7	advanced
8	unrestricted
9	copious
10	prosperity
11	life
12	paramount
13	controlled
14	typically
15	deities
16	temples

Test 5, pages 24-25
Human Brain

1	approximately
2	intricate
3	endeavour
4	organs
5	components
6	nervous
7	principal
8	mass
9	function
10	imagination
11	complex
12	navigate
13	hormone
14	prevent
15	generates
16	illuminate
17	recalling
18	connections
19	enhances

Test 6, pages 26-29
St Paul's Cathedral

1	recognisable
2	dominated
3	resplendent
4	plagued
5	reconstructed
6	engulfed
7	invasion
8	cathedral
9	calamitous
10	edifice
11	accomplishment
12	purported
13	alleged
14	spire
15	Monarchs
16	worship
17	conducted
18	unyielding
19	dilapidation
20	besieged
21	lightning
22	distinguished
23	dome
24	architecture
25	catastrophe
26	ravaged
27	charred
28	aftermath
29	commissioned
30	medieval
31	masterpiece
32	prodigious
33	prominent
34	ingenious
35	occupies
36	inscription
37	translates
38	notable
39	crypts
40	military

Cloze Tests: Partial Words

Test 1, pages 32-33

Fossils

1	impressions
2	palaeontologists
3	animals
4	evolution
5	quarries
6	sedimentary
7	solidified
8	revealed

Baboons

9	prevalent
10	discernible
11	patriarchal
12	transient
13	vindictive
14	reciprocal
15	terrestrial
16	vigilant
17	herbivorous

Test 2, pages 34-35

The Solar System

1	Scientists
2	billion
3	Solar
4	orbit
5	smaller
6	meteoroids
7	Jupiter
8	turbulent
9	spins
10	whirlpool
11	Earth

Piranhas

12	freshwater
13	rivers
14	camouflage
15	predators
16	powerful
17	reputation
18	ferocious
19	frenzied
20	piranha
21	scavenger
22	aquatic
23	humans

Test 3, pages 36-37

Vikings

1	hailed
2	adventure
3	history
4	seafaring
5	settled
6	fearsome
7	prolific
8	planks

Morse Code

9	transmitting
10	combination
11	pulses
12	information
13	communication
14	recognised
15	distress
16	amateur
17	Navy
18	naval

Cloze Tests: Partial Words

Test 4, pages 38-39		Test 5, pages 40-41		Test 6, pages 42-43	
The Ancient Olympic Games		**Braille**		**Mount Everest**	
1	Olympic	1	writing	1	soaring
2	festival	2	impaired	2	unparalleled
3	Greece	3	catastrophic	3	transcendent
4	dedicated	4	poked	4	traverses
5	Games	5	subsequently	5	collision
6	month	6	scholarship	6	substantial
7	city	7	experimented	7	instigated
8	athletes	8	fingertips	8	document
9	rules	9	invented	9	formidable
10	promise	10	system	10	abundance
11	ten	11	Soldiers	11	habitually
12	meant	12	comprised	12	hazard
13	wealthy	13	dashes	13	precipitously
14	event	14	rectangular	14	vigilant
15	stadium	15	miniscule	15	perils
16	time	16	arrangement	16	scarcity
17	boxing	17	distinguish	17	adverse
18	modern	18	represent	18	altitude
		19	punctuation	19	precarious
		20	word	20	numerous
		21	numerous	21	fateful
		22	special	22	summit
		23	typewriter	23	expedition
		24	Braille	24	proficient
		25	specific	25	glorious
		26	tangible	26	plateaus
		27	dedication	27	ascent
		28	visually	28	momentous

Other Titles in the First Past The Post® Series

Verbal Reasoning: Vocabulary

A good vocabulary is key to success in all 11 plus and Common Entrance exams. All exam boards use questions designed to test the candidates' vocabulary in both the English and Verbal Reasoning sections of contemporary multi-discipline exams. These books have been designed to improve the student's vocabulary through a focus on learning synonyms and antonyms. Full answers are included.

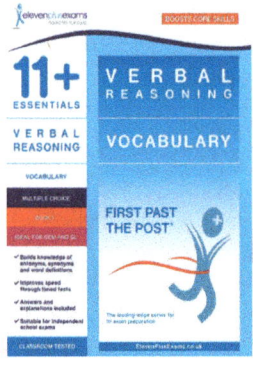

Each book covers several question styles in order to expose the candidate to as many as possible in readiness for the exam. In each book, there are several timed topic-specific tests and several timed mixed tests, which include several question styles.

Other Titles in the First Past The Post® Series

Verbal Reasoning: Vocabulary in Context

These books provide indispensable practice to help improve crucial comprehension and essential reading skills. Each page contains a short piece of text with five highlighted words, five example sentences with missing words and five definitions. The task is to figure out, using the context of the passage to help, which of the five highlighted words fit in which of the example sentences and which matches up with which definition. These books are not based on an exam-style format, instead they are designed to help build fundamental skills that are key to success in all 11 plus and Common Entrance English and Verbal Reasoning exams. Full answers are included.

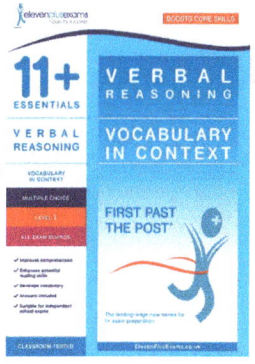

The books in this series come in four levels of difficulty, each level offering more challenging vocabulary than the last, to encourage development of comprehension abilities and confidence. Level 1 is the easiest, and Level 4 is the hardest.

Other Titles in the First Past The Post® Series

Verbal Reasoning: Puzzles

This puzzle series aims to test and improve the candidate's vocabulary in a fun and engaging way. A wide vocabulary is at the heart of all 11 plus and Common Entrance exams, and many question styles in the English and Verbal Reasoning sections are designed to test this. These books are filled with challenging crosswords and word searches which test over 700 synonyms, antonyms and homophones. Whilst being engaged in a fun activity, the candidate will widen their vocabulary with a selection of useful new words. Full answers are included.

Each book in this series contains puzzles which focus on each of synonyms, antonyms and homophones. Within each word group, there are puzzles at three difficulty levels. The final four puzzles on each topic are mixed puzzles, which feature all three word groups. It is easy to monitor progress and pinpoint areas for improvement with progress charts and word jotters.

Other Titles in the First Past The Post® Series

Verbal Reasoning: Vocabulary, Spelling & Grammar

These books have been designed to test and improve the candidate's verbal reasoning skills, especially their working knowledge of grammar and spelling and their vocabulary, which is key to success in all 11 plus and Common Entrance exams. Each book covers a large variety of question styles in order to expose the candidate to as many as possible in readiness for the exam. Full answers and explanations are included.

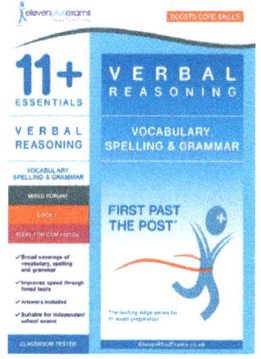

In each book, there are nine timed tests, each of which focuses on a specific question style, and a timed mixed test, which includes several question styles.

Other Titles in the First Past The Post® Series

Verbal Reasoning: Practice Papers (GL)

These books provide real exam practice via four timed tests. These are tailored towards the Granada Learning (GL) Verbal Reasoning assessments but provide invaluable practice for all exam boards. Each test contains a large range of question styles so that, over the four papers, all known questions styles that are likely to come up in the real GL exam are covered. The structure of each test is designed to reflect the likely make-up of the real exam. Full answers and explanations are included.

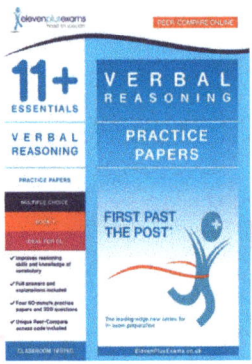

Each test can be marked and evaluated via our Peer-Compare Online system, which assesses the candidate's performance anonymously on a question-by-question basis. This helps identify areas for improvement and benchmarks the candidate's score against that of others who have taken the same tests.

Other Titles in the First Past The Post® Series

English: Practice Papers (GL)

These books provide real exam practice via four timed tests. These are tailored towards the Granada Learning (GL) English assessments but provide invaluable practice for all exam boards. Each test comprises a comprehension section and a spelling, punctuation and grammar section, reflecting the likely make-up of the real exam. Full answers and explanations are included.

Each test can be marked and evaluated via our Peer-Compare Online system, which assesses the candidate's performance anonymously on a question-by-question basis. This helps identify areas for improvement and benchmarks the candidate's score against that of others who have taken the same tests.

Other Titles in the First Past The Post® Series

Mathematics: Practice Papers (GL)

These books provide real exam practice via four timed tests. These are tailored towards the Granada Learning (GL) Mathematics assessments but provide invaluable practice for all exam boards. Each test covers a large range of topics so that, over the four papers, all known maths topics that are likely to come up in the real GL exam are covered. The structure of each test is designed to reflect the likely make-up of the real exam. Full answers and explanations are included.

Each test can be marked and evaluated via our Peer-Compare Online system, which assesses the candidate's performance anonymously on a question-by-question basis. This helps identify areas for improvement and benchmarks the candidate's score against that of others who have taken the same tests.